"God loves each of us as if there were only one of us."

The power of His words are reflected in this thoughtful collection of Inspirational Quotations.

"God grant me the serenity to accept the things I cannot change, the courage to change the things I can, and the wisdom to know the difference."

SR2

"As the sun creates your shadow, God creates your soul—but in each one it is you who determine the shape of it."

Frank A. Clark

"Love in your heart wasn't put there to stay.

Love isn't love 'til you give it away."

"God loves each of us as if there were only one of us."

SR6

"I know not where His islands lift
Their fronded palms in air;
I only know I cannot drift
Beyond His love and care."

Whittier

Footprints

"One night I dreamed I was walking along the beach with the Lord. Many scenes from my life flashed across the sky. Sometimes there were two sets of footprints, other times there was only one.

"This bothered me because I noted that during the low periods of my life when I was suffering from anguish, sorrow or defeat, I could see only one set of footprints, so I said to the Lord...'"

" '...You promised me, Lord, that if I followed you, you would walk with me always. But I have noticed that during the most trying periods of my life there has been only one set of footprints in the sand. Why, when I needed you most have you not been there with me?'

" The Lord replied, 'During your times of trial and suffering, when you see only one set of footprints, it was then that I carried you.' "

"God shall be my hope, my stay, my guide and lantern to my feet."

William Shakespeare

SR12

"Time flies, suns rise and shadows fall. Let time go by. Love is forever."

"It is not the body's posture, but the heart's attitude, that counts when we pray."

Billy Graham

"Life is fragile—
handle with prayer."

"Even if I knew, certainly that the world would end tomorrow, I would plant an apple tree today. For in the true nature of things, if we will rightly consider, every green tree is far more glorious that if it were made of gold and silver."

Martin Luther

"Be kind. Remember everyone you meet is fighting a hard battle."

T.H. Thompson

"Charity is twice blessed—it blesses the one who gives and the one who receives."

SR20

"We cannot hold a torch to light another's path without brightening our own."

Ben Sweetland

"Friendship flourishes
at the fountain of
forgiveness."

William A. Ward

"The best portion of a good man's life, his little nameless, unremembered acts of kindness and of love."

William Wordsworth

"The difference between a person and an angel is easy, most of an angel is on the inside, and most of a person is on the outside."

"Anna" age 9

"A Christian is a mind through which Christ thinks; a heart through which Christ loves; a voice through which Christ speaks; a hand through which Christ helps."

SR26

"Most of the shadows of this life are caused when we stand in our own sunshine."

Emerson

"I have 4 things to learn in life:
To think clearly without hurry or
    confusion;
To love everybody sincerely;
To act in everything with the
    highest motives;
To trust in God unhesitatingly."

Helen Keller

"To accomplish great things we must not only act, but also dream; not only plan, but also believe."

"Faith is adopting an orphan; it's buying without a warranty; it's paying in advance; it's traveling away from home with reservations."

Robert H. Schuller

"Doubt finds its life by digging in the cemeteries of buried hopes. Faith finds its life by scanning the horizon, knowing there will be a sunrise tomorrow."

Robert H. Schuller

"God gives us the ingredients for our daily bread, but He expects us to do the baking."

"The best and most beautiful things in this world cannot be seen or even touched, they must be felt with the heart."

"If you have lost faith in yourself, just go out and get acquainted with a small child. Win his love and your faith will come streaking back to you before you know it."

"Faith is the key to fit the door of Hope, but there is no power anywhere like love for turning it."

Elaine Emans

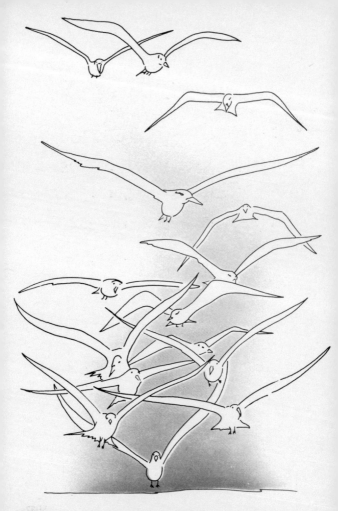

SR36

"God did not write solo parts for very many of us. He expects us to be participants in the great symphony of life."

"If you meet one too tired to smile,
Leave one of yours;
Nobody needs a smile, as much
as those who have none to give."

"You may be sorry that you spoke, sorry you stayed or went,
sorry you won or lost, perhaps, sorry so much was spent. But as you go through life, you'll find - you're never sorry you were kind."

SR40

"Has some misfortune fallen to your lot? This too, will pass away; absorb the thought, And wait—your waiting will not be in vain, Time gilds with gold and iron links of pain. The dark today leads into light tomorrow; There is no endless joy, no endless sorrow."

Ella Wheeler Wilcox

"A real friend warms you by his presence, trusts you with his secrets, and remembers you in his prayers."

"Pray as though everything depended on God. Work as though everything depended on you."

St. Augustine

"The three great essentials of happiness are:
   Something to do,
   Someone to love,
   And Something to hope for."

"Faith is not a
contradiction of reality,
but the courage to face
reality with hope."

Robert H. Schuller

SR46

"A heart full of joy and gladness
will always banish sadness and strife,
so always look for the silver lining
and try to find the sunny side of
life."

Jerome Kern

SR48

"Love is the fairest bloom
in God's garden."

SR50

"I shall pass through this world but once. Any good, therefore, that I can do or any kindness that I can show to any human being let me do it now. Let me not defer or neglect it, for I shall not pass this way again."

Anonymous

"Forgiveness saves the expense of anger & the cost of hatred."

Megiddo Message

"God wants us to be victors, not victims; to grow, not grovel; to soar not sink; to overcome, not to be overwhelmed."

William A. Ward

"I thank God for my handicaps; for, through them, I have found myself, my work, and my God."

Helen Keller

"Thank you, Lord, for the sheer joy of wanting to get up and help the world go around."

Roxie Gibson

"When life knocks you to your knees, you're in position to pray."

"Build me a son,
O Lord, who will be
strong enough to know
when he is weak, and
brave enough to face
himself when he is afraid,
one who will be proud
and unbending in honest
defeat, and humble and
gentle in victory."

Douglas MacArthur

"God holds us responsible, not for what we have, but for what we could have; not for what we are, but for what we might be."

"Give a man a dollar and you cheer his heart. Give him a dream and you challenge his heart. Give him Christ, and you change his heart."

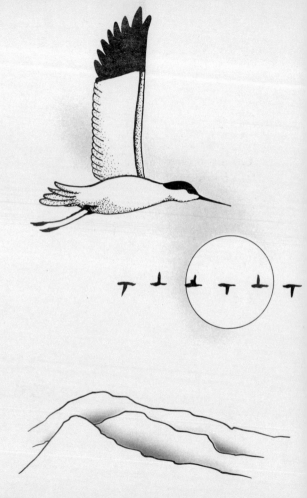

SR60

"Time is...
Too slow for those who Wait,
Too swift for those who Fear,
Too long for those who Grieve,
Too short for those who Rejoice,
But for those who Love,
    Time is Eternity."

"When you work for the Lord the pay may not be so hot, but you can't beat the retirement plan."

"The Christian life is not a way "out" but a way "through" life."

Billy Graham

"Character is what you are in the dark."

Dwight L. Moody

"Character is like a tree and reputation like its shadow. The shadow is what we think of it; the tree is the real thing."

Abraham Lincoln

"Constant kindness can accomplish much. As the sun makes ice melt, kindness causes misunderstanding, mistrust, and hostility to evaporate."

Albert Schweitzer

"Prayer provides power, poise, peace, and purpose."

SR68

"God makes a promise; faith believes it, hope anticipates it, patience quietly awaits it."

SR70

"It is better to master one mountain than a thousand foothills."

William A. Ward

"While faith makes all things possible, it is love that makes all things easy."

"A genuine Christian is like a good watch: He has an open face, busy hands, is made of pure gold, is well-regulated, and is full of good works."

"If a blade of grass can grow in a concrete walk and a fig tree in the side of a mountain cliff, a human being empowered with an invincible faith can survive all odds the world can throw against his tortured soul."

Robert H. Schuller

"When we reflect on the meaning of love, we see that it is to the heart what the summer is to the farmer's year. It brings to harvest all the loveliest flowers of the soul."

Billy Graham

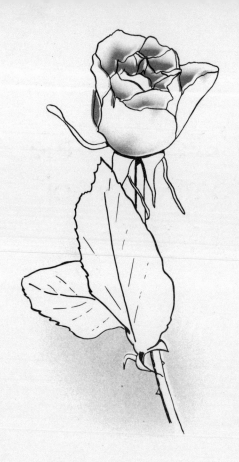

SR76

"Patience is the companion of wisdom."

St. Augustine

Other Great Quotations Books :

- Best of Success
- Business Quotes
- Commitment to Excellence
- Golf Quotes
- Great Quotes / Great Women
- Humorous Quotes
- Inspirational Quotes
- Loving You Is Easy
- Motivational Quotes
- Over The Hill
- Sports Quotes

GREAT QUOTATIONS, INC.
919 SPRINGER DRIVE • LOMBARD, IL 60148

TOLL FREE: 800-621-1432 (outside of Illinois)
(312) 953-1222